Hope Walks By Me

Justice & Liberty in the Lands of the Free

Hope
Walks
By
Me

Justice & Liberty in the Lands of the Free

Poetry and Prose by ex-offenders

Edited by Russ Litten and Josephine Metcalf

BARB
ICAN
PRESS

First published in Great Britain by Barbican Press in 2019

Funded by Arts Council England and Hull City Council.

Registered office: 1 Ashenden Road, London E5 0DP

www.barbicanpress.com

@barbicanpress1

Cover by Martin Lewsley at Atomluft

A CIP catalogue for this book is available from the British Library

ISBN: 978-1-909954-31-1

Typeset in Adobe Garamond

Typeset and Printed in India by Imprint Digital Ltd

Introduction

2019 marks the 25th anniversary of the release of *The Shawshank Redemption*, a prison film whose key themes of humanity and friendship have secured it a regular place in people's list of "best films ever". While the film is set in the fictional Shawshank prison (in real-life the former Ohio State Reformatory), there is a tendency to overlook that *Shawshank* is also about life *post*-prison. The film's official tagline, "Fear can hold you prisoner. Hope can set you free" can be applied to a whole host of situations outside of the prison. In the original novella by Stephen King, *Rita Hayworth and Shawshank Redemption*, Brooks was a minor character, though on screen he actually takes over the narration to talk about how difficult life is after release from prison. The film makes clear that even being provided with a job and housing cannot help Brook's tragic narrative. Indeed, on the outside, Brooks is "tired of being afraid all the time".

There is a whole plethora of problems facing prisoners upon release – not all ex-prisoners are as lucky as Brooks to be provided so readily with employment and accommodation. They face financial instability, familial complications, stereotyping from communities and an array of other difficulties that the average lay person might not consider (I too am complicit in this – I'm ashamed to admit that many years ago while working at a non-for-profit, I had reservations about hiring a recently released prisoner to do some administrative work for us). A number of people believe that a prison sentence itself is punishment enough; that any further challenges once released are hence unfair. For ex-prisoners, it regularly seems as if hope is quite literally walking by them.

Hope and conversely the hopelessness that comes with trying to maintain optimism in post-prison situations, underpins this collection of writings by people affiliated with Humbercare, Turning Point, and Restore & Resettle in Hull. All three organisations assist ex-prisoners with resettlement, enabling their service users to become integrated members of our communities in East Yorkshire. Most of the contributors to this collection have served prison sentences in the UK. Their creative writing was stimulated by weekly groups myself and Russ Litten started at these three centres. Russ is a local novelist who has spent many years as a writer-in-residence at local prisons and who also runs workshops at Youth Offender Institutes across the UK. As an academic in American Studies, I have particular teaching and research interests in representations of prison in (popular) culture – I believe prison films, memoirs, poetry, music can help us to understand US history, politics, and society more widely. I am also fascinated by the ways in which different audiences derive meaning from texts, especially when readers may themselves have experienced oppression or subordination in the form of imprisonment.

Russ and I conducted study and writing groups over the past several years. Among other texts, we all read memoirs by Shaun Attwood (a UK citizen incarcerated in the US for a number of years) and *Poems from Guantanamo Bay* edited by lawyer Mark Falkoff. We discussed Martin Luther King's infamous "A letter from a Birmingham Jail", listened to Johnny Cash's *Folsom Prison Blues*, and watched *The Shawshank Redemption, I am a Fugitive from a Chain Gang* and *Dead Man Walking*. But the discussion – as you will see in the following pages – evolved to incorporate questions of justice and liberty in the UK as well. Although US (prison) culture was our starting point, we delved into discussions of class, race, gender, citizenship, the economy, morals and immigration this side of the Atlantic too. These conversations then fed our creativity – for instance, poignantly writing "cup poems" (one line each) just as prisoners in Guantanamo Bay had done. We discussed the remarkable abilities of Guantanamo inmates as well as other incarcerated authors and characters to maintain hope in the face of such adversity.

This collection presents a sample of what we wrote (and deliberated) in these groups. Critical and creative production processes are complex at the best of times, let alone when faced with a range of barriers. Russ and I and the group members together negotiated low levels of literacy and the general disorder that comes from working with people who – often through no fault of their own – lead chaotic lives. But the satisfaction in witnessing the therapeutic power of reading and writing groups for these contributors offset any frustrations. We hope that these groups may have contributed – even if in small ways – to instil passions for thinking, reading and writing, as well as developing practical skills and life-awareness aptitudes. We are not so naïve as to think this process has radically reduced the risk of re-offending for those involved in the project, but we do hope that there may have been some element of sparking longer-term goals for redemption.

In closing, I must pass on my thanks to Russ – his enthusiasm, sense of humour, and ability to provoke fruitful discussion and writing is truly inspirational. We must also show gratitude to the British Academy, Arts Council England, and Hull City Council for making these groups possible. I am deeply appreciative of Martin Goodman for taking on this project with such interest; his Barbican Press with its promise to produce "books to challenge and surprise" is a perfect fit for these writings. And lastly, I'd like to thank the writers themselves, for sharing their experiences and opinions so honestly, and for their courage in converting them into verse and prose. So dear reader, before hope walks by you too, please read on and be challenged and surprised.

Josephine Metcalf, June 2019

KITCHEN, FRIDAY MORNING, 10:23 AM

What you doing? Writing? I've written bare poems, me.

Write us one, then.

Yeah, no problem. What about?

We're talking about America, prisons, the criminal justice system and that.

Fucking mad over there. You can get life for a bag of weed.

Sit down, tell us all about it.

Can't today. I'm busy today. But I will do, yeah, no problem. So what do you do, just talk about America?

Mostly, yeah. Stuff like the death sentence or hip hop or the war on drugs. And then we write about it.

Drugs? Don't talk to me about drugs.

Why?

Thing is, me, right, if I've got no money, I'm not bothered. I can just sit and chill. But if I've got money in me pocket, that's it. I can't stop till it's all gone. It's just rocks, rocks, rocks. When I've got money, I'm King for the day.

That sounds like the title to a poem.

I won't be here long, anyway. I've got a house, me, you know.

Yeah? Why aren't you in it?

She said if I carried on the way I am, I'll be dead by Christmas. But it's crack innit. As soon as I get some money, that's it. What can you do?

Write us a poem about that, then. Call it "King for a Day".

I will do, yeah. No problem. I'll do it tomorrow, yeah ...

Russ

1

HOPE

Hope walks by me
all dressed in green
the most beautiful sight
I've ever seen.

After seeing her
all my troubles
seem to just float away
like blowing bubbles.

Hope she comes to visit me
again one day
to brighten up my life
when all seems grey.

Mark B

DON'T FEAR THE NIGHT

You are the captain
of your soul;
seeking freedom
is your goal.

Hold on to that
ray of light;
no longer
will you fear the night.

Mark B

DEAR THERESA MAY
(after *MLK's Letter from a Birmingham Jail*)

Dear Theresa May,

I believe that the homeless situation in Hull is getting way out of hand. People will just walk on by and ignore any homeless person. They think "out of sight, out of mind". If we don't see it then it ain't happening – far from it, it's getting worse. Hostels aren't big enough or plenty enough to house everyone.

I have a suggestion that could work. Around England, there are many prisons that have shut down and are standing idle. These could be re-purposed into large hostels run by the government, even if only one, for now, could be rolled out for a trial period and if it works then on to the next one. They wouldn't even need much kitting out because all the basic facilities are there, all rooms with en-suite already.

I would very much appreciate it if you would look into this further.
I look forward to hearing from you soon.

Yours faithfully,

Mark B

GEORGE

Here's Old Man George,
down the gym.
Looking hench,
cos he's not thin,

keeping up
with the younger lads;
after the showers,
back to our pads.

I know George
isn't really his name,
but we'll keep using it
if it's all the same.

Mark B

BENETTON

When we went out
to do that job
we thought it would go well.
Little did we realise
the shop had got a bell.
The place lit up
amid a deafening sound,
we attracted bacon
from all around.
They said come here lads,
you're banged to rights,
it's down the station
for a couple of nights.
I thought I'd go no comment
and leave the pigs to guess,
but they seemed to know everything,
more or bloody less.
I couldn't understand it,
I never told them a thing.
Little did I realise
that you were going to sing.
Now when I got jail,
you got released and was out.
It finally came together:
you were the Old Bill's snout.
But I do believe in karma
and one day it will come;
I promise you some payback,
you no-good grassing scum.

Mark B

UP TOWN

Going up town
to spend my dosh,
off to M & S,
but it don't mean I'm posh.

Gonna call on Craig,
cos he needs to go as well,
he's off to Cash Convertors
to barter and sell.

Shouldn't be too long,
back in time for tea,
but if he drags his feet,
it will be only me.

Mark B

MY DEAR MUM

They say that hearts don't break, God,
but you know that isn't true;
the day you took my Mum away
you broke mine clean in two.

Look around your garden, Lord,
she'll not be hard to find;
she has a face that's full of love
and a heart that's good and kind.

Tell her that I love her
and when you see her smile,
please put your arms around her
and hold her for a while.

Mark B

MEMORIES ARE FOREVER

There's always a face before me,
a voice I'd love to hear,
a smile I'll always remember,
of a mother I loved so dear.

Deep in my heart lies a picture,
more precious to me than gold;
it's a picture of my mother,
whose memory will never grow old.

I don't ask for no miracles,
but today just one would do;
to leave my door wide open
and see my Mum walk through.

Mark B

WISDOM

Wisdom wears burnt orange
and has the brain of a child for breakfast.
They toddle off to the zoo,
where they work as a therapist to the monkeys.
When they get home to their treehouse,
Wisdom listens to heavy metal
before falling asleep in a red hammock
and dreaming of Camembert.

Group Poem

KINGS OF THE WORLD

America thinks it's King Of The World
and some of us think it's true,
we don't need them to fight our wars
because of the trouble they cause,
but reality bites when it's red, blue and white,
because of the stars and stripes.
They promise fast food and peace,
but the war machine kicks you in the teeth.
The land of the free,
but you get 99 years for being a thief.
America thinks it's King Of The World
but for most of us, it makes us hurl.

Group Poem

I AM NOT THAT KIND OF PERSON

I am not that kind of person
who says he cannot cope,
then the future will bring me happiness
for that it brings me hope.
I'll fly away from reality
and look for my own beliefs,
not joined by friends in the criminal world
from the murderers, druggies and thieves.
So what are your words of wisdom?
Or should I just elope?
Or should I just escape from reality
just by smoking dope?

Mark C

A LETTER TO MY "MASSA"

I've been fighting this so-called American Civil War for many many months and for what? White man power. Sold into slavery to fight for my freedom. I'm fighting for nothing. My colleagues are free, of course they're free – they're dead. Free from being a nobody and being humiliated by so-called friends who I'll be protecting in the line of fire. They say a soldier marches on his stomach. I march from scraps. My punishment is fighting this war.

Mark C

ESCAPE

My friends and inmates always say
I'm one of a kind,
the screws say I'm a good prisoner
cos they are hard to find;
even though I'm doing time
I have no choice in this matter,
so I'll get a job in the kitchens
to make nice crispy batter.
And now my time is over,
now I can go to my wife,
but if I find out she's been messing around,
next time I'll be doing life.
Now I need to escape from reality,
but the drugs are hard to find.
So don't do drugs, or anything,
and certainly don't do crime.

Mark C

DEAR SIR OR MADAM

I'm writing this letter understanding that the courts have remanded me in custody for some time now and now I've lost my job, my family and home for something I have not done. But time will tell if I'm guilty or not. If I am guilty I deserve to be punished, but if I am not guilty I might as well have been. Now I've lost my family life and home for your stupid mistakes by remanding me into prison.

But now I'm out. I'm in a hostel and now I'm incarcerated by Humbercare. So should I commit a crime so I can begin to do time on the outside?

Mark C

FROM DEATH ROW

I am sorry for what I have done
No one is with me now
I'm a lonely one
Now my time has come
My end is near
Seeing my victim's families
All I can do is shed a tear
I am separated from my children and wife
Only to know I've got minutes left of my life
The sound of electricity humming in my ears
Why do they do this to me?
Why don't they give me years?
So quiet please, everyone
Everyone shush
Stop talking, because here comes another one
A dead man walking
Soon not to be talking

Mark C

TO DEATH ROW

Of course you're sorry for what you've done
You should be executed for killing my son
I had two children, now only one
Your life is ending, mine's just begun
They could have put you in the state of correction
Now you will die by the lethal injection

Mark C

FROM THE BIG SCREEN TO THE BISCUIT

From Rocky to the Rocky Mountains
to the Vegas fountains
and everything in-between.
From the biscuit to the big screen,
from the Hard Rock Cafe to JFK,
to the flower of May,
from King Kong to Kim Jong,
from Central Park
to the Raiders of The Lost Ark,
it's all such a lark
to be shot in the dark.
From fast food chains
to Singing in the Rain,
from the man on the moon
to atomic boom.

Gavin

GUANTANAMO

(after *Poems from Guantanamo Bay*)

Is there love in Guantanamo?
I don't know.
If there was, where would you find it?
All it was for you was to get a hit;
with a gun in your hand,
you'd join the gang
and with a bomb strapped
to your body for the bang,
maybe you will get to hang.
But freedom you want
outside, to be with your clan,
you get nothing but torture;
is that your future?

Gavin

WASTED LIFE

(after *Redemption* by Stanley Tookie Williams)

Stanley, Stanley, what can I say?
Your life has been took away.
It must be hell in your cell,
not to see your family, far away,
wasted life, been took away,
all your friends, took away,
no fudge cake, McDonalds, took away,
no JD and Coke to drink,
oh you poor man, you must think
life is a bitch.
No music in your cell
or TV to watch,
hell is being in your cell,
no exercise, oh my God, it is hell,
being on Death Row, in your cell.

Gavin

20

KITCHEN, FRIDAY MORNING, 11:13 AM

She says she just wants to move to another city, somewhere where she can start again. Somewhere posh with nice people and nice shops and no druggies or alkies or people taking advantage. Somewhere you can go for a nice walk and you don't get hassled by scum. She says there's too many weird people in Hull. She went to America once, when she was little. She went with her Mam and Dad. Florida. She met Mickey Mouse. It's hard to remember it all now, so much has happened since then. Writing it down helps. Getting going is the hardest bit, she says, but once that pen starts moving, she can't stop.

Is it right to turn a prison into entertainment? What do we think about that?

Let's get it down, he says. Let's get it all down on paper. He says the great thing about creative writing is you can't get it wrong.

Everyone is quiet now, pen to paper. She's back there again – the palm trees, the ice cream, Mickey Mouse. She can feel the sunshine on her face. She's ten years old again.

Someone bangs on the window, voices shouting outside, and all heads come up.

We're back in the room.

Russ

FRAGMENTS OF AMERICA

They go in there to the Middle East
and death and destruction is the only thing released.
They leave, same as the UK, when the destruction has gone wrong;
why oh why did they release the bombs?
So the Middle East is still the same,
us and America are to blame.

America as the fast food chain,
they do everything big and we are nearly the same,
the wars they entered are never fulfilled.
God bless America in all it tried to do,
we don't need to learn lessons from you.

America, they use too many guns,
they shoot, I think, just for fun.
We do the same in smaller ways;
America has not seen happy days.

I love American films,
but they are eccentric, just to give us thrills.
I love America,
but not their ways,
so I will leave that country to yesterday.

Robert De Niro plus Tom Cruise,
the films they make are breaking news.
I love their music,
Slim Shady is my best.
I think it's because the rap he makes
means sense.

Angela

WINGS

Why do you do these cruel things?
If only this slave had wings
he could fly away,
not be harmed in any way,
have food and have drink
and a better life, I think.
The slave leader is cruel in many ways,
I wish all this cruelty would end one day
and generations to come
would not hear about it in this way
and there would be nothing left to say.

Angela

MIND GAMES
(after *Escape from Alcatraz*)

Alcatraz is the worst place on Earth for these prisoners
and America should be ashamed of their barbaric treatment
and the government of America, they are the criminals,
their cruel mind games,
but the American government don't think like me and you,
so maybe it's going to happen again one day;
another prison of torture with no values,
so the prisons in America may be the same again.
God bless America for causing people this pain –
it's insane.

Angela

A LETTER TO THE PRIME MINISTER

(after *MLK's Letter from a Birmingham Jail*)

To Theresa May, the Prime Minister of England

Why do you lie so much, promising Brexit for the people of England and not delivering the goods? I celebrated when the People's Vote was the right one, it was my birthday on Brexit day in Birmingham. I celebrated by watching the great news. Why do so many Eastern Europeans live in England? They say they're here to work – that may be true, but most love the cash machines of England, while you help fewer Muslims that are left to die in the cold seas with very brutal ways of fleeing war, risking their lives and their children's lives.

You selfish bitch, I hope you rot in hell for this shit.

Yours,

Angela

TO THE PRESIDENT

Please can you pardon me?
I only killed three.
They pretend my family broke my trust
and that was fucking enough,
I put the bullets in my automatic gun
that I never use just for fun;
my family are my life,
I never meant to end their life,
but my family comes first
and now I'm on Death Row,
facing the worst.
Please, Mr President, can you pardon me?
This is my final plea.

Angela

ANGEL

You are my angel child,
with your wings
you can travel far and wide
to pastures new,
into a better life,
no one can stop you
from doing what you want to do,
so aim for your dreams
and always respect you.

Angela

SUNDAY

Sunday, I took a stroll in the park;
some scum walking towards me
I know from Westbourne House.
I was so exposed and vulnerable
with my mobile in my hands.
They tried selling me things
but I said no to them.
One of them was waiting
to take my phone, but in the park
their opportunity did not come,
so they said come to our house
and me, like a sheep to the slaughter,
I did.
They put my phone upstairs on charge
but I knew I should not have been
in the company of scum;
One of them said his friend had
run out with my phone,
but I knew I was risking maybe my life;
I was alone.
He tried to lure me up the street
but I knew then I would be beat.
I made a bad mistake.
I got on the nearest bus in heartbreak;
I don't want to live in fear,
walking the Hull streets, thinking they're near,
so when I get my chance
I will go to another city
and take a chance of a fresh start –
I think I will sing and dance.

Angela

A BETTER WAY

I'm worried all the time,
I rarely smile,
I'm worried about court,
I feel abandoned, on my own,
no one to turn to,
nowhere to go.
But things have to get better,
no more worse,
I feel like I've been given
an external curse.
He said I'm an ugly English bitch,
why doesn't he fuck off back to Portugal?
I wish he never came my way
but in a hostel, things happen this way,
so I will leave in a few weeks from today.
I hope to God my life turns out
in a better way.

Angela

INCIDENT IN MARKS & SPENCERS

Off to town to spend some dosh
in Marks & Spencers,
thinking I'm really posh;
they say get out, you scruffy dog,
I throw all the knickers on the shop floor,
they say don't come in here no more
or we will bounce you out the fucking door.
Went to town to spend my voucher,
the staff said fuck off you sloucher.
I was crying back on the bus,
I met a guy called Russ;
he said give me that voucher,
don't kick up a fuss.
I gave him the contents of my card,
he said I need it cos I work really hard,
I'm running low on butter and eggs,
he said go earn your money
by selling some pegs.

Angela

I REMEMBER

I remember the smell of fish and chips being fried
I remember Bess eating her carrots
I remember my mother's touch
I remember never seeing my Dad
I remember standing alone
I remember my Granny always being there
I remember feelings of being all by my self
I remember loss
I remember hurt
I remember anger
I remember pain
I remember crying
I remember my mother's smell
I remember nobody cares
If I live or die
I remember hate
I remember it's just me

Elizabeth

THE CRAZY LIFE (always)
(after Luis J Rodriguez's memoir, *Always Running*)

Always waking up thinking
that this will be the day of change.
Having nothing,
always trying to survive.
Collecting all my goods
in a black bin bag,
never quite seeing the light,
always swimming upstream,
having the taste but
never being able to swallow.
Always having the horrible
feeling in the pit of my stomach.
Always hearing noises while
my imagination runs wild.

Elizabeth

PLEASE FIND PEACE

(after *They Fight for Peace, Poems from Guantanamo Bay*)

Please find peace
you keep talking the talk
but no fighting
keep calm, your plan is set.
Peace, they say;
walk the walk
but don't do the talk.
They kill because
they have nothing else
to do except fighting with you.
To kill is not simple;
keep the fight for peace.

Elizabeth

THE JUSTICE DONKEY

What is justice?
Justice to me
is the doling out of punishments
to liken the act committed,
giving likewise punishment.
My image of justice
is a donkey
with uneven weights on either side.

Side to side,
side by side,
step by step,
no steps to the side,
the weight we'll carry,
equal on sides;
until justice is carried,
equal weights will reside.

Trevor

MY LIFE

I stand by the altar,
there can be no fault, yeah,
except my own.
Sometimes wish I was a clone,
pitted like a drone,
except now I stand alone,
feeling the punishment through my bones.
Smashed, cut, split and shattered,
my mind now is just matter,
I feel like the Mad Hatter,
it's justice on a platter
with a rope in front of me,
no more harder it will be,
just a jolt
and I'll be free –
just one day in the life of me.

Trevor

HAPPINESS

Happiness is a gingerbread house in a tree
where he slots down cream buns
one, two, three;
happiness is a Mexican town by the sea,
drinking cocktails and feeling free.

Group Poem

TO WHOMEVER
(after *Poems from Guantanamo Bay*)

Where shall I begin?
I know of you,
from what I have
shall I say heard
and watched on
international and worldwide news.
We know what has happened
to you all.
What to say to you?
Where do I begin,
when we do not know
you at all?

Jackie

THINK

When brought into the world
we start with education
to learn about the right and wrong
of the nation,
to learn about the foundation of life.

The attraction of doing better
brings the interaction of people
we want to be.
Come with the complexion
and a bit of fascination
will bring the knowledge you seek.

People struggle to do the things
that are right
cause the best things in life
are the ones that come with a fight.

See the configuration of your confrontation
will keep us away from probation,
now correction will lead people's
expectation
of you being no longer
in Incarceration.

You wanna do well in life?
Well, do have patience,
be your own badman
of your own co-operation,
don't let the contamination
of others bring you down.

See, now put contraception on
the temptation of doing bad,
the good of life can't be that sad.

Life will bring a little competition
but in comparison being the good
ain't that embarrassing,

Yo, contemplation comes from consideration
of others we don't need to fight for;
we're all like brothers,
we all came from the same place
– our mothers.
Now be good role models to our youngers.

Yo, completion of this crime
and this sentence, I've done my time,
if you wanna rob then think of these words
in this rhyme and think it ain't mine.

Shaun

HANDCUFFS AND A CHOKE HOLD

Yo, just another look in the mirror
but I don't really see what my face
can tell me,
there ain't a lot to tell G,
ya just another locked door & cell key,
just another locked gate
with a prisoner behind it screaming
"out… somebody help me".
That's right, I'm trying to work
the hand Satan dealt me
and hope this rhyme don't fail me.
I write with emotion,
though I don't know if all this
lyrical pain is healthy,
but I gotta keep the author's truth
even if it means speaking the awful truth;
that's the real sound
"round here", a smile so scarce cause
there ain't much to laugh about,
yo, that's right, a couple suicides
and that's no joke,
a couple times the razor blunt
or the rope's broke,
so they try again, cause something
inside of them says
life ain't worth living in handcuffs and a choke hold.

Shaun

SHINING

Faith says there ain't no hope,
the years, months and days seem to go slow,
training days means there's no rec time,
like to think there ain't much I don't know,
like to think to the depths most people won't go
like to think I can play the same it's
fucked (in both holes),
the system's fucked (low blows),
got fucked up by the screws (broken nose),
so sat here on my lonely, just me
and my own ghost;
is it that I see what most don't see, or I
see what most won't?
On the other side of the fence, feels like
I no longer know home,
see I've dropped a lot, now they embrace my fall,
the only thing I ain't made fall is Governors,
but my name rings bells for Governments;
I done banging, hyping, assaults and fighting,
I've done smash ups, done wilding,
done shutting it down, I'm done rioting,
done rooftops, I'm done climbing,
got nothing left to prove,
I'm always shining.

Shaun

CREW

Killing time, time, time,
you will be yours or will be mine,
you know the score, in this Crew,
after all, you're not brand new,
everyday you're not brand new,
if you want to be part of this Crew,
head held high and hand held low,
you know which way you got to go.

Mark Y

MOTOWN HOUND

Bobby Brown kicked out a tune for Motown
The city that never sleeps is in its dressing gown
The city is an apple and it's big and it's round
Fifty spat a verse and now he's getting down
Fifty states with many western towns
Bound to howl like a Motown hound

Group Poem

MISSING YOU

I thought of you today,
but that's nothing new.
I thought of you yesterday,
but that's nothing new.
And the day before that
and tomorrow too,
I'll be thinking of you
all through my life,
because I really do miss you.

Wally

UNIQUE

My hair is tracked,
can you find the lines?
Look for me in there
and you will only get stuck
in a curl.
My eyes are blue,
think with a tint of white.
Don't you think they tell you
anything?
Our bodies are unique,
all different shapes and sizes.
What can they teach you?
What do they show?
Life is a mystery,
we always change and grow.
Where have they been?
Where will they go?

Brad

NO MEANS NO – KEEP MOVING

No means no, because I know
who I am and who
I would like to be.
If we spread our wings
would we fall or fly
free?
How would you know behind
the eyes of another's seen?
Don't lose yourself, but
run faster – see, life
is a rose that you
have to keep soft.
You know me;
not so starkly,
tread carefully, please
save a heart as they
break so easily.
Holding so many will
make it harder to be.

Brad

KNOWING YOU

How well do we translate?
How well do we decipher you?
How well do you see within
your four walls?
To see your mind is one
in a million,
looking for light in dark
places is hard, love
and light is the hardest.
Fight. How strong minded do
we need to be to hold
ourselves in place?
You see. Why do you
think we turn to God?
He's just a key that is
invisible.
Do you think it's through fear
of not pulling the power
to push? I don't mean to offend his name, but he
opens doors we fail to
claim and we're left sat
without any answers.

How bad was your pain?
Was it in your mind?
Could you show me scars to horrify?
Being locked in a box
could be the same as not knowing
where to turn.
People's minds hide in fear,

but I would see your words
and I know we're colour blind.
Soft voices aren't bad,
but what do you hide?
Life isn't bad,
but it's what we leave behind.
Crying isn't weak – it's what we do.

If I sat with you, would you ever open up?
I wouldn't push you,
but how else do we know
what's running through?
Being natural is good,
but can lead you anywhere.
Life shouldn't be controlled
or forced.
We need to learn to stand ourselves up,
learning to say no is good,
but does that put you under threat?
See your own power, you are strong.
Voices cut deep, just so you know,
I don't like to be numb,
but some people believe
they are pushed down too far
or lost in the fact you can't face yourself,
don't like the ego.
Go straight to the heart;
the soul is stronger than you know.

Brad

REMEMBERING

I remember getting told off at
Primary school for swearing. 4 years old.

I remember riding my electric police
bike to school.

I remember making a skidding patch
at school by putting water down.

I remember saying the Lord's prayer
every morning in assembly.

I remember school meals
(enough said).

I remember ringing the school bell
for break times.

I remember drinking ice-cold milk
with a straw.

I remember going to secondary school
next door to primary school.

I remember running across wet, soaked
fields doing cross country at school.

I remember my first girlfriend, and going
abroad to Majorca for the first time.
I remember breaking up, and crying for weeks;
she was my first proper girlfriend, my first love.

I remember leaving school 6 months early, 15 years old,
because I had a full-time job to go to – £66 a week!

I remember the first time I smoked weed;
I was in Bass House in town, 14 years old. I was too young to drink.

I remember the first time I smoked heroin; I wish I'd never started.
The girl who introduced me to it died. She was 23 years old.

I remember being very very upset when my dad died.
7 months later, my Mum died.

I remember going to prison for the first time,
20 years ago.

Christian

LIFE IS CRAZY

(after Luis J Rodriguez's memoir, *Always Running*)

Life is crazy,
life is wild,
life is hard.
Every day, sometimes the same,
we trudge along in vain.
There's only you who can change it;
one minute you're up, then you're down,
sometimes a smile, sometimes a frown.
Some people are nasty, they call you a clown;
you have to get along, not all the time,
there's only you who can change your life.
I want to be settled, maybe find a wife,
I know I'll get there, one day soon.
I lay on my bed and stare at the moon;
I need a job to occupy my mind,
I keep on looking, but never do find.
I could do more, but sometimes it feels
so much like a chore, I know I could
do a hell of a lot more.
When my head is straight, no more crap,
I'll go out there and find me a job,
something I like, but I'll probably need a bike,
bank some money, keep away,
get a place, never to stray.
I want a life, better than this,
because sometimes it feels
like people take the piss.

Christian

A GUN AND A BIBLE

Here I am, all alone
the thoughts, going through my head.
If only I hadn't fired that gun,
I wouldn't be here.
I wouldn't be sad and unhappy.
But it's too late,
the damage is done;
I just have to get on with it,
one day at a time.
I find comfort reading my Bible;
I might find answers,
I might not.

Christian

BE STRONG, MY BROTHER

(after the poem 'Hunger Strike' in *Poems from Guantanamo Bay*)

I know it's up to you
if you refuse food,
but what good are you dead?
You are no good to anybody dead
Maybe you can bargain with your captors?
Probably not.
But please start eating
so at least you can pray
in your cell when lights go out.
But it's up to you –
whatever you think is best.
The truth will come out some day.
Be strong, my brother

Christian

THE KEY
(after *Poems from Guantanamo Bay*)

Dear Sami al Haj,
I am writing to you with regards
to your poem
it really touched my inner spirit
I am not religious
but I understand every word of yours.
You have been made to suffer for nothing
and I am so glad you have found some way
to make it through your daily torture.
Be strong –
survival is key.

Peter

YELLOW STICKERS

Off in town to blitz our money,
virtual coins, sweet like honey.
A tent for Angie,
some food for Mark,
a lamp for Jason,
cause he's scared of the dark.
M&S is where we'll go,
past all them outside smoking blow,
the spice we want comes in racks
and not outside in dosser's slacks.
Fill our bags with yellow stickers,
hand them out to window lickers,
we're feeling happy, feeling good,
we always knew we could.

Group Poem

KITCHEN, FRIDAY MORNING, 11:42 AM

He talks like a poet, but he doesn't want to write anything. What's the point? What good is a poem, or a story, or anything made up? It doesn't solve anything. It doesn't make anything better.

He likes books, though. He has a book he found in a charity shop – The Devil's Dictionary, by Ambrose Bierce. We dip into it and read some of the entries out loud. They are dripping with tar-black humour and vitriol. He's a funny fella, this Ambrose. The great and good would sidle behind pillars when Ambrose licked his pencil.

Why don't you write something like that? they say. He just laughs. What for? What's the point? I mean, I know it makes your life easier and helps you with your project or whatever it is, but what then?

OK, she says, you say the lines and I'll write them down.

He just smiles and shakes his head.

Her pen hovers over the paper.

What ever happened to Ambrose Bierce? Nobody knows for sure. In 1913 he rode into Mexico with Pancho Villa, and nobody ever heard of him again.

Russ

YOU DON'T WANT ME INSIDE YOUR HEAD

You don't want me inside your head,
I will talk you into swallowing your own tongue.
You need a dictionary to deal with me
and my sense of camaraderie.
My gang is called *Asbestos Dos Trios;*
the name was relevant at the time.
My friends and I share so much,
but time moves on and I accept that's fine.
Working at the tip, the day it flooded
the vicars kept arriving with books to ditch;
I searched their rubbish, books so old,
I peeled their pages and got my fix.

Anth

HISTORY AND THE PEOPLE WHO MAKE IT

I love truisms, philosophical truisms
and words that explain themselves.
I read the dictionary and soak it up,
the father of all medicine in my cup.

Gibbons was a genius, alive at the time of King George,
he wrote history that everyone should read.
He went to Oxford, and Cambridge University
and caused a furore, he spoke of diversity.

I'm fascinated by those debating houses;
I know my history and know my facts.
This man, his doctrine, was make do with less
but the people weren't sure it was so fresh.

These Franciscan monks enjoy the banquet halls;
we dip into the feast and dip out the open window.
It's the way to liken life – in and out;
I'm here, that's enough to spout.

Anth

JUSTICE

Why do we wear blindfolds?
Things are about to be revealed
in the name of justice,
in the name of balanced justice,
being chopped up and thrown down
the whaler's stairs,
Ii was their form of justice,
but that wasn't justice, was it?
Nor is it to be thrown from the Tarpeian Rock.
There is only one community in the world with no crime
and one punishment for all crime
(leave and don't come back).
But surely that's not justice either?
Is it justice or sadism?

Anth

NOT A PRETTY PICTURE

My hair is nothing but trouble.
My nose is perfectly non-descriptive.
My years are in an appreciation society.
My neck could be famous.
My shoulders are camels – no, wait, donkeys.
My arms are shoplifting arms – a five finger discount.
My body is past its sell-by date.
My body will soon be done with the business of breathing.
My fingers are digits – fly away Peter and Paul.
My legs are scaffolding poles.
My feet are hooven – like the goat.
My toes are like strings of pearls.

Anth

THE ROBIN

The robin that flew through the banqueting hall
grazed the top table for bread.
He hopped past the fire and fluffed up his wings
and sang "nothing can ever be dead".

Group Poem

IF I WERE A JUDGE FOR A DAY

(after *Poems from Guantanamo Bay*)

I'd be the meanest judge in the world to those who deserve it.
I'd pass out sentences and just wouldn't care.
I just can't imagine it, it would not happen.
I'd send the bad men and women away forever.
I'd project them to the geographical consciousness of Australia.
I'd wear a purple wig and a clown suit,
a feather duster for my gavel.
I'd execute at 4 in the morning, like they did in Rome.
I'd ask myself at the end of the day
If I served a fair justice.

Group Poem

WHAT MATTERS MOST IS HOW WELL YOU WALK THROUGH THE FIRE
(after Charles Bukowski)

Today was the day when the entire village would know the true Sufi. Feeling the heat of the fire, he didn't know where he would land. He could hear the crowd on the other side of the tent, a babble of laughter and the caterwaul of his mother on the other side of the village. "If for no one else," he thought, "I have to do this for her. Is my heart strong or will it burst in the middle of the flames? Will my legs buckle and turn to cinders?" Sufi emerged from the tent blinking in the soft glare of the torchlight. The moon and stars were questioning his next move. The jailer pushed him forwards prodding his back with a stick. The North Star never moved, but beckoned him with haste. The corridor of fire was already ablaze, dancing like pale horsemen. He stepped up gingerly, closed his eyes, and heard his mother's cry once again. "My mother," said Sufi and he charged. The flames leapt and the cries fell away.

Anth and Brad

NOT BELIEVED

I close my eyes and you haunt me
Your image I can't bear
I hate this world that surrounds me
When I felt you there

I hate the way you touched me
Who the hell gave you the right
To treat me like you wanted to
To take advantage every night

I was only 8 when I felt the touch
Of your ugly hands that I hate so much
I never knew why you did this to me
Why I was the one no one believed

You left me feeling stupid and shame
Somehow you made me feel I was the one to blame
Did I really deserve this from someone I trusted
I thought you were blood but my body you lusted

I close my eyes and you still haunt me
This image I can't bear
I hate that you surround me
Even though you're not there

Jason

DEPRESSION

Depression is running through my head
These thoughts make me think of death
A darkness which blanks my mind
A walk through a graveyard is what I find

Black shadows walk between the graves
How many lives have not been saved
Six feet under, if not more
How do I go down and explore?

The feeling of lying in a box
I can't get out, is it locked?
Is it day or is it night?
Are birds singing or bats taking flight?

I know one day this is where I'll go
Am I afraid? I don't think so
Will I be able to explore feelings of death
Long after I have taken my last breath

Jason

FALLING FROM DARKNESS

Falling from darkness
To a place I don't know
Everything moving with no place to go
I feel so alone and so so scared
As I fall I wonder, is anyone there?
As the days and nights pass right by
I count the hours as I lay and cry
Falling from faith, falling from love
Is there anyone there, anyone above?
Never did I want to feel like this
When the answer lies with a slit of the wrist
My mind is racing to find a solution
Before it's too late and I'm just an illusion
No one knows how I really feel
I just want someone to hold me and help me heal
As I fall I feel the rain
And realise this is not the way to ease my pain

Jason

INDEPENDENT LIVING

Sat in the garden feeling so alone
Feeling tired, untidy, smelly and dirty
Not even having a phone
Down in the dumps
In a bad state of depression
Not making a good first impression
Walking through the door
Not knowing what to expect
Greeted by a lady called Hannah
Who spoke to me in a good manner
Sat in reception waiting to be assessed
Not knowing what to say – I feel so depressed
A few hours passed by as I started
To feel a bit more at ease
Just wanting to eat some toast with cheese
Most people can cope while others fail
Everyone is different, we all have
Our own story and tale
I find things so hard – it's hard to explain
Cause my days now aren't the same
My heart is bursting with pain again
For such a long time
I've been part of this place and house
Now living independently
Like a little lonely mouse
I'm just sad and lonely
No interest in making this place homely
It's hard to adjust after such a long time
Stuck here in this place of mine
My confidence has gone

I'm back to square one
As night time falls,
I feel trapped in these walls
The loneliness starts to begin
The fear and anxiety kicks in
Lots and lonely
In this cold dark place
Not wanting to be here
In my own space

Jason

POEM FOR ANDY

(after *The Shawshank Redemption*)

What does hope really mean?
Is it just a pipe dream?
Hope can be dangerous
Can drive a man insane
If time could have gone on
The same could have happened
To Andy Dufresne
In all the years at Shawshank
There have been less than ten men
Who I believed when they told me they were innocent
Andy Dufresne was one of them
Andy came to Shawshank in 1948
He was a 30 year old who looked like a toad
He was a short neat little man
With sandy hair
But didn't really seem to care
And small clever hands
That did a lot of scams
He wore gold rimmed glasses
His fingertips were always clipped
And they were always clean
He collected rocks and limestone most of the time
He shaped and polished them
To a high shine
Is he really innocent?
We may never know
Guess we will have to see
How things go
Listening to the lady sing

Is when his escape plan begins
We all face pain
But not everyone is the same
Brooks took care of Jake
Until he could fly
To help time pass by
He fell out of a nest
Brooks did his best
Andy ended up down the block, in the hole
Like a dosser on the dole
Andy Dufresne crawled
Through 500 yards of crap and grime
To escape from doing time
He came out clean on the other side
Shortly after he took himself for a ride
He got hold of a rock hammer
And broke free from the slammer
To the Pacific Ocean and tide
He fixed up his old boat on the side
He made it look like new
All he needed was his crew
To laugh and joke
Cos they outsmarted a screw
Red met up with Andy at the Pacific Ocean
And their plan was set into motion
They looked back at their time in detention
When Andy Dufresne escaped
From Shawshank Redemption

Jason

MODERN SLAVERY

We hear about modern slavery
Each and every day
These people want their work done
But just don't want to pay
They prey on us weak and vulnerable
And control us in every way
With punishment and humiliation
Through each and every day
Rations of food
Punishment and crime
Which victims of modern day slavery
Suffer most of the time

Jason

LIFE WITHOUT LOVE

A heart has feelings, well, what would that be?
For I love just the thought of you
And I hope you feel the same for me
Life without love is an emptiness
I'm not sure I wanna face
Because I know that time
Will never be able to erase
I wish our love was simple as a sunset
Ready to be born again
But I know in truth
Love only comes from within
So I'll keep watching for my sunset
Looking for that rainbow to shine someday
Then one day maybe our love
Will find its own way

Jason

ABUSE

Evidence of pain
As you hear her cry your name
There's nothing you can do
He hurt you too
You yell "Leave me alone"
He hits her again and again
Causing severe pain
Let's just leave, you say
But there's nowhere to go
Cards you weredealt
Wounds heal slow
A life you don't want
You cry and fight back
It's no use
Just horrible abuse
You become used to it
Not knowing another way
But becoming his prey
Living to fight for another day

Jason

I MISS YOU

Every day I wonder why
You were taken up to the sky
And I didn't get a chance to say goodbye
There are so many things I want to say
That every night I sit and pray
Hoping you can hear me say
I miss you and love you
Each and every day
There's so much hurt I feel inside
And in nobody can I confide
I know you are watching over us
Up above where the angels lie
You're in our hearts
And there you'll stay
And be remembered
Each and every day

Jason

HUMBERCARE

I've spent so many times
At Futures and Dock House too
At first not knowing
What to do
Lost, lonely and in fear
Sick of wiping
Away the tears
Slowly starting
To build up trust
Whilst still fighting
To adjust
They help to take
The stress, pain and fear away
Allowing you to feel free
And fight to get through
Another day
The staff are so loyal
And so true
In all they say
And do
When staff leave
I go and cry
As it's so hard
To say goodbye

Jason

GREEN MILE

Standing in the window
Dreaming what will be
Realising all that's been lost
Not knowing what is to be
You hear the cell doors open
You know it's not your turn
The only thing you can do
Is smell the others burn
Fear, anger, stress and pain
Nothing more for me to gain
I sit here like I'm forgotten
Just an old crook
Left to go rotten
I stand in shame
Knowing I'll only walk
The green mile
Once again

Jason

NO TWO DAYS

Keep hope in your heart
And don't let it part
Hope is like a crystal
Rare, precious and bold
I know this from stories
That I've been told
Hope is what makes us
Human in our soul
Each day that comes and goes
Each night that passes by
Is just another step
For our hopes to come by
Hope and fear
Stress and pain
No two days
Are ever the same

Jason

ALCATRAZ
(after *Escape From Alcatraz*)

It stands as a monument of fear
A torturous exhibit near
To San Francisco's high elite
Their snickering was indiscrete
I wonder did they sail around
The prisoners that had been bound
Who wallowed in their lifeless cage
With little hope into old age
The walls and floors have ageless stains
Of blood and beatings, all their pains
They echo into the minds of men
To not allow such grief again
The paranormal shows agree
The torture goes on endlessly
Though no more does a breath abide
Within these walls, deep dark inside

Jason

I AM A WRITER

I came to Hull in 2014
It was the first time
I'd seen or ever been
My journey started in William Booth
For the first couple of months
Things ran real smooth
Then I was faced with a bit of hell
Anxious, depressed, not knowing
Who to talk to or who to tell
Cold and lonely, deep inside
Sick of finding places to hide
Not knowing what to decide
Thinking of my dignity and pride
I'd sit in the park
Feeling like there was a hole in my heart
Fear, stress, grief and loss
Felt like some didn't give a toss
Grief is something
That's hard to get though
Don't let it defeat you
Wanting to place
Deep thoughts in my heart
With intentions of making
A brand new start
Facing fear, stress and pain
Having to go through it all again
Stress, tension, much more
But not to mention
Best left behind a closed door
Moving places all the time

Just wanting one I can call mine
Hostel life can be very mean
I know, with some of the things I've seen
Some call us tramps, thieves or dossers
But we don't care
At least we're not tossers
To some it's like home
With staff like family
Not like them cowards
Who lived in Bramley
Humbercare have been my rock
With care and support
Around the clock
The staff are amazing
In all that they do
I felt I needed
To share this with you
I woke up this morning
It was foggy
I went to the garden
And there sat Oggy
Live your dreams
Follow your heart
Make the best start
Build confidence in your heart
Life can be mean
And very unkind
Don't let depression
Play on your mind
Stay confident, see things through
Do the best things for you

Keep strong, be a fighter
And one day you
Could be a creative writer

Jason

LOST CHILD

When I look back at my life and all the abuse I faced, sometimes it hurts and feels like it was yesterday. Though these past few years have been the worst, when I write it brings a mixture of the fear and upset pain, but also makes me feel strong. I suppose it's more like a way of coping and trying to understand more.

If I can be honest, the worst time was during his long trial, with the loss of my partner not very long before, so yes, it was hard.

A lot of people would have crumbled or fallen apart.

But the way I saw it, I wasn't willing to let him win.

My future with him behind bars needed to begin.

I lost my partner and then with this, all emotions running wild.

Still feeling like a lonely lost child.

Jason

ONE NATION

To walk alone but to stand together
Down the boulevard of opportunity
Walking through any kind of weather
To the land of hope and liberty

Fresh air and sunshine all around
No laws, no weapons, no discrimination
Felling safe together on the same ground
Everyone becoming just one nation

Group Poem

JUSTICE

Justice is an ugly thing
Unless the sentence fits the crime
Sometimes the judges get it wrong
Time in jail can drag on
Incarceration is a nightmare
Call doors banging, keys jingle jangling
Expect more than you will get – jail is something you just won't forget

Group Poem

MARTIN LUTHER KING

Making waves in the black community
Acting proud of the right to be free
Raising awareness of the racist mindset
Tricky whites see him as a threat
Injust, unjust, it was all just wrong
New black leader garnered an enormous throng

Most of the cause centred on Jim
Angered blacks seeking to target him
Rooted in the southern cause
They sought equality for unjust laws
Inspiring millions, they achieved much more
Noting poverty and war they also bore

Group Poem

AMERICA

Twin towers blown up
Al-Qaeda in the frame
Bush is in the White House
Who is truly to blame?
Going to war for nothing
Where did it begin?
Are we truly righteous?
Or do we live in sin?
Skyline construction
Towers above
Heavens fade to darkness
Where is the light of love?
Let's all meet in Central Perk
Gather all our friends
Greet each other with no status
All the different blends
Of broken hearts
And broken souls
Unite us together
Towards a common goal.

Group Poem

CHAIN GANG

(after *I am a Fugitive from a Chain Gang*)

Churning out workers
Hard labour in the sun
Angry men and women
Impossible to run
Never ending work day
Grunting through the pain
An image of lost loved ones
Never will be the same
God help me and help us all

Group Poem

GLORIFY

Chopper, Charlie, Reggie & Ron
We used to have heroes and now we have none
A set of values warped and misshapen
To the heavens they are taken
They put them on a movie screen
Big them up in a fantasy scene
Hold them up for all to see
Showing us all what not to be
Where does fantasy end and fact begin?
Is it so great to be living in sin?
Is the average guy too boring to star?
Across the nations near and far
Who is truly worthy of fame?
Does the criminal life just cause pain?

Group Poem

INCARCERATION
(after *Public Enemy*)

I'm stuck in the system I can't get out
I didn't do nothing but they don't have a doubt
I'm strung up, hung up, set up to fail
Because I'm the wrong colour I'm not allowed bail
I can't remember what I'm in here for
Gimme a way out, show me the door
Sort out the system, it just doesn't work
Trigger happy officers, they just go berserk
Don't get me started on the money they make
They've earned a lot off me to this date
Release me, feed me, give me a vote
I won't come back I promise I won't.

Group Poem

THE AMERICAN DREAM

Is America really there?
Or is it a lucid dream?
A matrix of a happy despair
This situation is not as it seems
The vets who sleep out on the streets
The poor who line up for the stamps
The history that always repeats
Reservations of holiday camps
Are all of these things just up on the screen?
An illusory land of the free
Visions of America largely unseen
A Mickey Mouse conspiracy.

Group Poem

DEAR MUHAMMAD

(after *Poems from Guantanamo Bay*)

I'm sorry to see that a child
as young as you
can be locked up
with no sign of release.

Only 14 years old
terribly tortured and beaten
for what reason?
They act like
you've committed treason.

One day you shall find
your freedom,
back with your family
bet you can't wait
to see them.

All I want to say is
one day you are going to be OK
the tides will turn, now
you're having your say.

David

THE LIGHT
(after *Poems from Guantanamo Bay*)

O prison, open your gate,
as I love the light.

Here in prison, I sleep
through the darkness

and open my eyes to
the light.

The world and its bliss
will be there on your release.

A boy may despair in his problem
where a man will learn and do well.

Those who persist will attain their goal
A boy, a man, and a woman an'all.

God will see you through.

Shane

BOTTLES ON THE SHELF

It's the clanking of the bottles that makes people stare,
They're whispering and pointing, but she's not aware
She turns the key quietly as she doesn't want disturbing
Then lays baby in bed, for now it's still sleeping
Stumbling hard, she falls over the stool
Who put that there, you stupid bloody fool
La la la la, she sings a little song
I need a drink, she thinks, that's not so wrong
One bottle, two, maybe three or four
Who's that knocking at the bleeding door?
She sees movement in the cot, the baby awakes
Not just yet honey, give Mammy a break
Her whole life's a shambles, a complete mess
Oh what the hell, she wipes beer from her dress
Are you in there, someone yells?
I bet you're pissed, the whole bloody landing smells
The baby is crying and people can hear
Oh please don't cry like that, my sweet little dear
I only meant to have one, then it got to seven
Please end all this God, and take me to heaven
Where's those pills, I must do it myself
Then there'll be no more bottles left on the shelf
Come on darling, you must come with me
It'll be OK, you wait and see
Here, I've done yours, drink your drink
My head's spinning, I can't think
Bang on the door, the handle is turning

What's going on in there, the baby stopped crying
She turns to look, oh God, they're right
I'm sorry my angel, my poor little mite
I never meant to harm you without myself
I only wanted to clear the bottles off the shelf

Lynn

HOPE IS

Hope was my nana's maiden name,
she married into Atkinson, but she
remained the same.

Hope is something
that we cling onto.
Hope is different
for me than it is for you.
So cling
on to what you have and hope for
what you haven't

Hope is something that we own from birth
Right through to heaven.

Shane

HOPE IS A WEARY TRAVELLER

Hope is a weary traveller
It comes and goes, like a bad taste in your mouth
One day everything can be going north for you
The next it could be south.

Hope is a light at the end of the tunnel
It's like a dream; when you reach for it
It moves further and further away
It's faster than the speed of light
It will never ever stay.

Hope is like the American Dream
You see yourself in the next few years
You know what you want to do
You have no fears.

But hope can turn around on you
So be sure to keep your guard
Cause if you find yourself disappointed
You're going to find it hard.

Anonymous